BABAR'S CHOICE

Adapted by
Lesley Young

HAPPY BIRTHDAY POM, FLORA AND ALEXANDER said the banner stretched across the banquet hall. Pom and Flora were there, but where was Alexander?

Suddenly he popped up from under the table. "Hello," he said. "Are you having fun?" Then he ducked under the table again and emerged at the other end beside three of his elephant friends.

"Are you having a good party?" he asked. "Keep my seat - I'll be back in a minute."

"What's Alexander up to, then?" Celeste asked Babar.

Just then he appeared, out of breath. "I've - puff - got a problem," he panted.

"I promised to sit next to my friends," explained Alexander. "But then I found out I was meant to sit beside Flora and Pom."

"Why can't you tell your friends?" asked Babar.

"I'll hurt their feelings," said Alexander. He sat down sadly. Babar sat beside him and put an arm round him. "Let me tell you what happened to me, long ago, when I was young..."

It was the day of the palace ball. Zephir bounded into Babar's bedroom and called out, "Are you nearly ready?"

"A drum roll please!" shouted Babar from behind a screen.

As Zephir beat a drum roll with two candlesticks on a globe of the world, Babar strode from behind the screen to reveal his dinner suit - which was about ten sizes too big!

"Is that what they mean by 'fit for a king'?" asked Zephir.

The royal tailor arrived and threw up his hands in horror when he saw the suit. He pulled it off Babar, spinning him like a top.

"I hope he gets it right *this* time," said Zephir, laughing.

Just then Cornelius lumbered in, looking very worried. "This is awful," he moaned. "Who decided to seat the Gorilla King next to Baron von Boar? They've been feuding for years!"

"I did," said Babar. "I thought they might make friends."

"A good idea," said Pompadour, "but it could be disastrous!"

"Then why don't we sit the Gorilla King next to the Koala Queen?" said Babar.

"It's too hard to explain," said Pompadour. Babar gave up trying. "*You* decide," he said to Pompadour.

"Now, about your schedule for this evening," began Pompadour.

"You will meet your guests at eight o'clock," continued Cornelius.

"Including your escort for the evening," smiled Pompadour. "The Gorilla King's daughter, the lovely Princess Midge."

"What? But I've invited Celeste to the ball!" cried Babar.

"My tusks, Babar!" exclaimed Cornelius. "The Gorilla King is our guest of honour. His daughter *must* be escorted by you."

Babar collapsed into a nearby chair with a sigh. Then he leapt up again with a yell - he had sat right on the flowers he was going to give Celeste! It just wasn't his day.

Babar didn't know what to do. Should he escort Celeste or Princess Midge to the ball? He decided to go and see the one person he could always rely on for good advice - the Old Lady.

In her sitting room, Babar found it easy to explain the problem. The Old Lady sat in her favourite chair and listened to him.

"As King, it is my duty to take Princess Midge to the ball," said Babar. "But I've already promised to take Celeste, my friend."

"You will have to decide between the two," said the Old Lady. "But remember, your true friends will always understand. Honesty is the best policy."

Babar sighed. "I know what I have to do."

Babar then went to see Celeste. "Babar, what are you doing here?" she exclaimed when he and Zephir arrived at her house.

"It's about the ball," began Babar.

"I can't wait. We'll have a great time, won't we?" said Celeste.

"Well, maybe," said Babar, "then again, maybe not..."

"What do you mean?" she asked.

"Um...," said Babar. "It's - it's..."

"Well, tell me!" said Celeste.

"It's - your flowers," said Babar. "I - er - sat on them."

"Is that all?" sighed Celeste. "For a moment I thought you were going to say you couldn't take me to the palace ball."

"Now you mention it..." he began.

"I'm sorry, Babar, I've got lots to do," said Celeste. "Thanks again for asking me," she added. "You're very kind."

"And completely spineless!" remarked Zephir, as they left.

Babar went to look for Cornelius to confess his problem, but before he had a chance Cornelius said, "Before you begin, I would just like to remind you how important tonight is."

"But I haven't..." started Babar.

"It's vital that you get on well with Princess Midge," continued Cornelius, "then the elephants will have better relations with the Gorilla King."

"But I must tell..." tried Babar.

"I know," smiled Cornelius, "it must have been hard to explain it all to Miss Celeste."

"But I didn't..." squeaked Babar.

"Thank you for putting your duty first," finished Cornelius.

Babar gave up. "Don't mention it."

Arthur, Babar and Zephir sat watching the staff preparing for the grand ball. "Only a few hours to go, and I'm still taking two people to the ball," sighed Babar.

Arthur was looking closely at two apples he'd grabbed from a passing fruit cart. He was trying to decide which one to eat. At last he said, "When in doubt, take both."

"That's it!" cried Babar. "Well done Arthur - I'll take them both to the ball!"

At last evening came. Cornelius and Pompadour greeted the Gorilla King and the Princess Midge.

"I am so glad you could grace us with your presence," said Cornelius.

"Ugh!" replied the Gorilla King.

Pompadour got out his phrase book of *Gorilla Grunts* and flicked to the 'Ugh' section. He translated, "His Majesty says he is most pleased to be invited." He looked at the book again. "Or, it could be that His Majesty is bored."

Princess Midge was growing very restless. She wanted to start the dancing with Babar.

"Look," said Cornelius, "He's just coming down now." Everyone turned to see Babar, Arthur and Zephir at the top of the stairs.

"His Most Royal Highness King Babar!" announced Pompadour.

Zephir whispered to Babar, "As I suspected, Celeste is late. You are free to greet Princess Midge."

"But how did you know she would be late?" asked Babar.

Arthur and Zephir exchanged smiles. "I hid her shoes," chuckled Arthur.

Babar made his way regally down the stairs.

"King Babar," pronounced Pompadour in his most pompous voice, "It is our extreme pleasure to introduce you to His Royal Majesty, the Gorilla King. And this is his daughter, Princess Midge."

The formal introductions were suddenly interrupted as Celeste came weaving her way through the guests towards the palace steps.

Everyone stood back, clearing a path for her, straight to Babar.

Babar stood with one hand extended towards the Gorilla King, a smile frozen on his face. Things were looking very tricky.

At that moment a long, hairy arm reached over and yanked Babar off his feet.

"I hope you've got plenty of energy for dancing," said Princess Midge.

Babar grabbed her and spun her out on to the dance floor.

Then Celeste came up, but before she could say a thing, Babar stuffed a rose between her teeth and waltzed her outside.

"Celeste - let's tango!" he cried.

When Princess Midge realised
that she had somehow lost Babar
she soon came looking for him. She
spun back and crashed into the
dancing pair, sending Babar
reeling. He landed in a heap at the
Gorilla King's feet and watched as
Princess Midge and Celeste waltzed
past him.

When the Princess saw her
mistake she dropped Celeste and
ran back to Babar. She grabbed
him and began throwing him out at
arm's length, then pulling him
back. Then she missed again, and
yanked in a surprised-looking
Arthur instead of Babar.

Babar took the chance to collapse
on to a chair beside Celeste.

"There you are!" she cried, pulling
him back on to the dance floor.

"I'm getting very dizzy," thought
Babar, as he whirled around.

Princess Midge soon lost Arthur, so she looked around for Babar. Suddenly she thought she'd spotted him. "Here I come," she shrieked playfully, charging at a Babar-shaped shrub and pulling it up by its roots.

Babar watched in amazement as she danced off with it. Just as he had breathed a sigh of relief, the princess saw him. She threw down the shrub and ran at him. Babar tried to run off, but she caught him with a party streamer.

Zephir managed to cut the streamer, and Babar spun back into the seat next to Celeste.

"Oh, you're back," she cried. "We really must dance!"

"I don't think I can carry on like this much longer," thought Babar.

And so it went on, with Babar shuttling about between Princess Midge and Celeste. At last the princess flung him forwards with more force than usual and Babar went hurtling through the air, landing in a heap at Celeste's feet.

Desperately, he looked around and saw a drinks trolley nearby.

"Punch?" he asked Celeste, lamely.

"Don't tempt me!" she snapped, and walked angrily away.

At that moment, Pompadour stepped forward to make an announcement.

"Ladies and gentlemen! Gather round. King Babar will now crown his own choice of Belle of the Ball!"

"Oh no!" cried Babar, as both Celeste and Princess Midge sidled up to him.

"I don't know how you're going to get out of this one," said Arthur.

The crowd held its breath - who would he choose?

To everyone's surprise, Babar walked past Princess Midge and Celeste. They all gasped as he placed the crown on the Old Lady's head.

"The Old Lady will always be the Belle of the Ball for me," he said.

"Thank you, Babar," said the Old Lady. "May I have this dance?"

"Of course," said Babar, but out of the corner of his eye he could see Celeste turning sadly away.

As they danced, the Old Lady asked Babar what was troubling him, and he explained.

"I just didn't want to hurt anyone's feelings," he finished, "but I'm not being fair to Celeste, or Princess Midge, or even Cornelius."

"So, what are you going to do?" said the Old Lady, smiling.

"Tell Celeste the truth," he replied.

The Old Lady kissed Babar. "I'm proud of you," she said.

Babar found Celeste sitting sadly by herself and explained. "It was my royal duty to take the Gorilla King's daughter to the ball," he said, "but I tried to take you - as well."

Celeste laughed, "You should have told me, silly! You did it because you wanted to make me happy."

They looked over to where Princess Midge and Zephir were dancing furiously. "It looks as if the Princess has found another partner," smiled Celeste.

"And I've found mine," said Babar.

"So - you went through all of that for nothing!" said Alexander.

"Yes. If I'd told the truth in the first place I could have saved myself a lot of trouble," replied Babar.

Alexander thought for a moment. "Hey - maybe I should try that! If they're friends, they'll understand."

"Of course they will," said Babar.

And, of course, they did!

Based on the animated series
"Babar"
a Nelvana-Ellipse Presentation,
a Nelvana Production in Association
with The Clifford Ross Company.

Based on characters created by
Jean and Laurent de Brunhoff.

Carnival
An imprint of the Children's Division
of the Collins Publishing Group
8 Grafton Street, London W1X 3LA

Published by Carnival 1990

ISBN 0 00 193225 X

Printed in Great Britain by
BPCC Paulton Books Limited
This book is set in New Century Schoolbook 14 point